W9-BKL-560

My United States

Minnesota

MARTIN SCHWABACHER

Children's Press®
An Imprint of Scholastic Inc.

Content Consultant

James Wolfinger, PhD, Associate Dean and Professor
College of Education, DePaul University, Chicago, Illinois

Library of Congress Cataloging-in-Publication Data
Names: Schwabacher, Martin, author.
Title: Minnesota / by Martin Schwabacher.
Description: New York, NY : Children's Press, an imprint of Scholastic Inc., 2018. | Series: A true book | Includes
     bibliographical references and index.
Identifiers: LCCN 2017057589 | ISBN 9780531235614 (library binding) | ISBN 9780531250808 (pbk.)
Subjects: LCSH: Minnesota—Juvenile literature.
Classification: LCC F606.3 .S393 2018 | DDC 977.6—dc23
LC record available at https://lccn.loc.gov/2017057589

Photographs ©: cover: St Paul Minnesota MN/Alamy Images; back cover bottom: Wildnerdpix/Shutterstock; back cover ribbon:
AliceLiddelle/Getty Images; 3 bottom: Wiskerke/Alamy Images; 3 map: Jim McMahon/Mapman ®; 4 left: Edgar Lee Espe/Shutterstock;
4 right: Katerina Kovaleva/Dreamstime; 5 top: JoeChristensen/iStockphoto; 5 bottom: GREG RYAN/Alamy Images; 7 top: Wildnerdpix/
Shutterstock; 7 center top: JB Manning/Shutterstock; 7 bottom: PBouman/Shutterstock; 7 center bottom: Saibal/Getty Images; 8-9: Matt
Anderson Photography/Getty Images; 11: Tom Thulen/Alamy Images; 12: Visual&Written SL/Alamy Images; 13: Jim Mone/AP Images; 14:
Jim Brandenburg/Minden Pictures; 15: Universal Education/Universal Images Group/Getty Images; 16-17: Henryk Sadura/Shutterstock; 19:
CRAIG LASSIG/AFP/Getty Images; 20: Tigatelu/Dreamstime; 22 left: Alexander Zavadsky/Shutterstock; 22 right: Drawbot/Shutterstock; 23
center left: Julia_Lelija/Shutterstock; 23 bottom left: Tatiana Popova/Shutterstock; 23 center right: Katerina Kovaleva/Dreamstime; 23 top
left: Edgar Lee Espe/Shutterstock; 23 top right: Oliver Hoffmann/Shutterstock; 23 bottom right: critterbiz/Shutterstock; 24-25: Minnesota
Historical Society/CORBIS/Getty Images; 27: Underwood Archives/age fotostock; 29: Education Images/UIG/Getty Images; 30 right:
Map of the Louisiana Purchase, 1926 (engraving), American School, (20th century)/Private Collection/Photo © GraphicaArtis/Bridgeman
Images; 30 left: Underwood Archives/age fotostock; 31 top left: Minnesota Historical Society/CORBIS/Getty Images; 31 top right: Ivan
Dmitri/Michael Ochs Archives/Getty Images; 31 bottom right: Alexander Zavadsky/Shutterstock; 31 bottom left: Education Images/UIG/
Getty Images; 32: Minnesota Historical Society; 33: NICHOLAS KAMM/AFP/Getty Images; 34-35: GREG RYAN/Alamy Images; 36: Andy King/
Getty Images; 37: JoeChristensen/iStockphoto; 38: Ariana Lindquist/Bloomberg/Getty Images; 39: ZUMA Press Inc/Alamy Images; 40 inset:
Chris Oberholtz/Kansas City Star/MCT/Getty Images; 40 background: PepitoPhotos/iStockphoto; 41: KiraVolkov/iStockphoto; 42 top left:
Bettmann/Getty Images; 42 top right: George Rinhart/Corbis/Getty Images; 42 bottom left: Alexander Zavadsky/Shutterstock; 42 bottom right: Minnesota Historical Society/CORBIS/Getty
Images; 42 bottom right: AP Images; 43 top: ZUMAPRESS.com/age fotostock; 43 center right: Ben Margot/AP Images; 43 center left: DEZO
HOFFMANN/REX/Shutterstock; 43 bottom left: Mark Brettingen/Getty Images; 43 bottom center: Kevin Terrell/AP Images; 43 bottom right:
Andrew Harrer/Bloomberg/Getty Images; 44 bottom left: Minnesota Historical Society; 44 bottom right: Daniel Thornberg/Dreamstime;
44 top: Milen Mkv/Shutterstock; 45 top left: pixhook/iStockphoto; 45 top center: Deyan G. Georgiev/Shutterstock; 45 top right: Fiskness/
Dreamstime; 45 bottom: Wildnerdpix/Shutterstock.

Maps by Map Hero, Inc.

Front cover: Saint Paul Winter Carnival

Back cover: Canoer on Cross Bay Lake

Welcome to Minnesota

Find the Truth!

Everything you are about to read is true **except** for one of the sentences on this page.

Which one is **TRUE**?

T or F The weather in Minnesota is cold year-round.

T or F Minnesota contains the northernmost point in the United States outside Alaska.

Find the answers in this book.

Key Facts

Capital: Saint Paul

Estimated population as of 2017: 5,576,606

Nicknames: Land of 10,000 Lakes, North Star State, Gopher State, Bread and Butter State

Biggest cities: Minneapolis, Saint Paul, Rochester

UNITED STATES

Minnesota

Contents

1 Land and Wildlife

2 Government

THE BIG TRUTH!

Honeycrisp apple

What Represents Minnesota?

Showy lady's slipper

4

Minnesota State Fair

Hmong girl in
traditional dress

5

This Is Minnesota!

CANADA

Lake of the Woods

Rainy Lake

Boundary Waters Canoe Area Wilderness

Grand Portage National Monument

Red River Valley

Rainy

INTERNATIONAL FALLS

Upper Red Lake

Lower Red Lake

Minnesota Discovery Center

1

Superior Upland

LAKE SUPERIOR

Paul Bunyan and Babe the Blue Ox

BEMIDJI

NORTH DAKOTA

Red

2

Lake Itasca

GRAND RAPIDS

Forest History Center

DULUTH

MOORHEAD

MINNESOTA

BRAINERD

Mille Lacs Lake

Lake Superior Marine Museum Association

Runestone Museum

Mississippi

St. Croix

3

ST. CLOUD

WISCONSIN

Minneapolis Institute of Art

ST. PAUL

SOUTH DAKOTA

MINNEAPOLIS

Minnesota

AMERICA

Mall of America

Historic Fort Snelling

Science Museum of Minnesota

Pipestone National Monument

4

MANKATO

Jolly Green Giant Statue

ROCHESTER

Transparent Man

Mississippi

0   50
Miles

IOWA

1 Boundary Waters Canoe Area Wilderness

This protected wilderness area in northeastern Minnesota contains more than a thousand lakes. Visitors can paddle their canoes for days while hearing nothing but the sounds of nature.

2 Lake Itasca

At this small, northern lake, the mighty Mississippi River begins its 2,350-mile (3,782-kilometer) journey to the Gulf of Mexico. Surrounding the lake is a state park where visitors can enjoy the wilderness.

3 Minneapolis Institute of Art

For over a hundred years, great art from all over the world has been displayed at this museum in Minnesota's largest city. There is also a world-class children's theater next door.

4 Pipestone National Monument

Native Americans have long used the stone collected at this site to carve sacred smoking pipes. Visitors can enjoy nature trails and more.

Lake Superior is the largest freshwater lake in the world.

CHAPTER 1

Land and Wildlife

Minnesota is known as the Land of 10,000 Lakes. This might sound like a lot, but there are actually even more lakes than that! The state has nearly 12,000 lakes that are 1 acre (0.4 hectares) or larger. Minnesotans love their lakes. In summer and fall, they go swimming, fishing, and boating. In winter, when the lakes freeze over, they go skating and play hockey. They even fish through holes in the ice.

Ice and Lakes

Thousands of years ago, Minnesota was covered by enormous **glaciers**. As the glaciers expanded southward, they carved up the landscape. The moving ice scraped the state's northern regions clean down to the **bedrock**, carving holes that later filled with water to become lakes. Southern Minnesota is covered by dirt that the glaciers pushed along, creating rich farmland. When the glaciers melted, more lakes formed between the piles of dirt and rock left behind.

This map shows where the higher (orange) and lower (green) areas are in Minnesota.

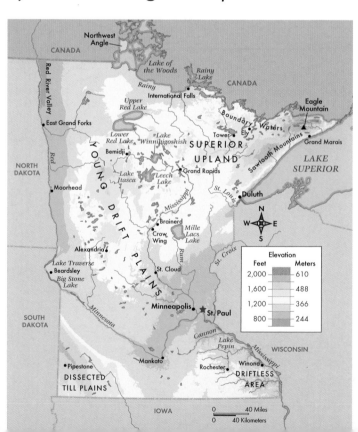

Mille Lacs Lake

Minnesota's second-largest lake, Mille Lacs Lake, was named for the lake-filled region around it: *mille lacs* means "1,000 lakes" in French. Thousands of boaters enjoy this lake in central Minnesota during the summer.

In winter, people drag 5,000 fishing huts onto the lake, creating a town called Frostbite Flats. They cut holes in the ice to go ice fishing—sometimes from inside heated huts. Ice fishing contests can draw thousands of people.

Ice fishing huts are heated inside, but the floor is the frozen surface of the lake.

Lake of the Woods spans from Minnesota into the Canadian provinces of Ontario and Manitoba.

Northwest Angle

CANADA

Lake of the Woods

Area of map

MINNESOTA

Way Up North

Minnesota contains the northernmost point in the United States outside Alaska. A notch in the northern border, called the Northwest Angle, spans the massive Lake of the Woods. On the far side of the lake is a chunk of Minnesota that is bordered on all sides by Canada. Lake of the Woods contains 14,552 islands and 65,000 miles (104,607 km) of shoreline.

Cold Weather

Minnesota is famous for its long, cold winters. It gets so cold in wintertime that the cities of Minneapolis and Saint Paul each built 5 miles (8 km) of "skyways." These enclosed walkways allow people to walk from building to building without going outside. In summer, however, the state gets extremely hot and humid. It's perfect weather for jumping in a lake to cool down.

MAXIMUM TEMPERATURE
115 °F

MINIMUM TEMPERATURE
-60 °F

The Minneapolis Skyway System is made up of pathways that connect 80 city blocks.

Fields and Forests

The northern third of Minnesota is covered with forests that attract hikers, campers, and hunters. Pine, spruce, and fir trees keep some forests green year-round. Other local trees, such as birch, oak, and maple, drop their leaves each winter.

The southern two-thirds of the state is part of the Great Plains. It was once blanketed by tallgrass prairies. These wild grasslands have been almost entirely replaced by farms. Minnesota's many wheat and dairy farms have earned it the nickname the Bread and Butter State.

The white bark of the paper birch tree was once used by Minnesota's Native American people to make canoes.

More than 2,800 gray wolves live in Minnesota today.

Wild Animals

Minnesota's lakes are filled with fish such as northern pike, walleyes, and muskellunge. They're also home to ducks, geese, and loons, the state bird. Deer, beavers, bears, and wolves roam the northern woods. Wolves used to be seen as a threat to farm animals. People killed so many wolves that they became **endangered**. Wolves are now protected and have started to come back in larger numbers. They help maintain a natural balance by keeping the state's deer population under control.

The Minnesota state capitol's marble dome is modeled after St. Peter's Basilica, a huge church in Rome, Italy.

CHAPTER 2

Government

Minnesota's capital is Saint Paul. The state's biggest city is Minneapolis, which is located right next to Saint Paul. Together, the two are known as the Twin Cities. They are located where the Minnesota River meets the Mississippi River.

Saint Paul began as a small town called Pig's Eye Landing. Its location on the mighty Mississippi was as far north as steamboats could travel on the river before they had to turn around.

Three Branches of Government

The three branches of Minnesota's state government meet and work in the state capitol. The governor heads the executive branch, which sets budgets and manages state workers. The legislative branch includes representatives from all over the state. They form the House of Representatives and the Senate, which create new laws. The judicial branch is made up of the state's judges, who interpret state laws.

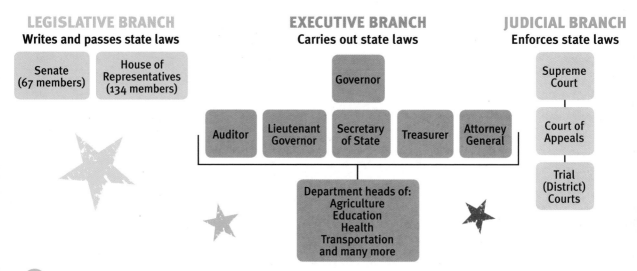

MINNESOTA'S STATE GOVERNMENT

LEGISLATIVE BRANCH
Writes and passes state laws

| Senate (67 members) | House of Representatives (134 members) |

EXECUTIVE BRANCH
Carries out state laws

Governor

| Auditor | Lieutenant Governor | Secretary of State | Treasurer | Attorney General |

Department heads of:
Agriculture
Education
Health
Transportation
and many more

JUDICIAL BRANCH
Enforces state laws

Supreme Court

Court of Appeals

Trial (District) Courts

In 1999, voters elected a governor from neither major party. Instead, they chose Jesse Ventura, a former professional wrestler.

Party Time

Minnesota voters do not always follow the traditional two-party form of politics that governs most of the nation. Instead of Democrats, the state has a Democratic-Farmer-Labor Party (DFL). The DFL formed when the Democratic Party merged with the Farmer-Labor Party, led by farmers, miners, and other workers. The state's Republican Party changed its name to Independent-Republican (IR) from 1975 until 1995 to appeal to independent-minded voters.

19

Minnesota in the National Government

Each state elects officials to represent it in the U.S. Congress. Like every state, Minnesota has two senators. The U.S. House of Representatives relies on a state's population to determine its numbers. Minnesota has eight representatives in the House.

Every four years, states vote on the next U.S. president. Each state is granted a number of electoral votes based on its number of members in Congress. With two senators and eight representatives, Minnesota has 10 electoral votes.

2 senators and 8 representatives

10 electoral votes

With ten electoral votes, Minnesota's voice in presidential elections is about average compared to other states.

The People of Minnesota

Elected officials in Minnesota represent a population with a range of interests, lifestyles, and backgrounds.

Ethnicity (2016 estimates)

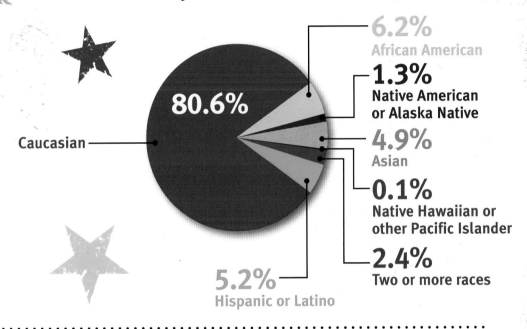

80.6%
Caucasian

6.2%
African American

1.3%
Native American or Alaska Native

4.9%
Asian

0.1%
Native Hawaiian or other Pacific Islander

2.4%
Two or more races

5.2%
Hispanic or Latino

71% own their own homes.

6% are veterans.

8% were born in another country.

34% have a bachelor's degree or higher.

93% of the population graduated from high school.

11% speak a language other than English at home.

What Represents Minnesota?

States choose specific animals, plants, and objects to represent the values and characteristics of the land and its people. Find out why these symbols were chosen to represent Minnesota or discover surprising curiosities about them.

Seal

Minnesota's state seal shows a Native American on horseback and a white settler plowing a field. An axe and tree stump represent the clearing of forests for lumber and farms. The state motto, *l'etoile du nord*, appears on a banner. It means "The Star of the North" in French.

Flag

The state flag shows a version of the state seal against a bright-blue background. The seal is ringed with showy lady's slippers, the state flower. The flag includes three dates: 1819, the year Fort Snelling, the first permanent U.S. settlement in Minnesota, was built; 1858, the year Minnesota became a state; and 1893, the year the first state flag was adopted.

Wild Rice
STATE GRAIN
This wild grain has been collected by Native Americans for centuries. It is now also farmed, and Minnesota is one of the leading states in wild rice production.

Showy Lady's Slipper
STATE FLOWER
These delicate orchids grow in bogs and swamps. They are so rare that it is illegal to pick them.

Honeycrisp Apple
STATE FRUIT
Originally bred at the University of Minnesota, the Honeycrisp is now one of America's most popular apples.

Walleye
STATE FISH
The walleye is one of Minnesota's most popular—and tasty—fish.

Common Loon
STATE BIRD
No Minnesota lake is complete without a pair of these beautiful diving birds. Their haunting call sounds like ghostly laughter.

Ice Hockey
STATE SPORT
In winter, Minnesota's frozen lakes become natural hockey rinks.

NOT PRIVILEGE BUT JUSTICE

Members of Saint Paul's Vote for Women Club pose for a portrait in the early 1900s.

The Nineteenth Amendment to the U.S. Constitution was passed in 1920, granting women the right to vote.

24

CHAPTER 3

History

Minnesota has been a U.S. state since 1858. But by this time, groups of people called Paleo-Indians had already been living there for about 10,000 years. Even before the glaciers finished melting, people roamed the northland, hunting **woolly mammoths** and other animals. Their **descendants** settled in the area and developed unique cultures.

Prairie People

On the prairies, the Dakota people farmed corn, beans, and squash. They also hunted bison with bows and arrows. They lived in portable, cone-shaped tents called tipis. These homes were made of wooden poles and bison hides. Tipis could be taken apart and rebuilt quickly, making them perfect for easy travel.

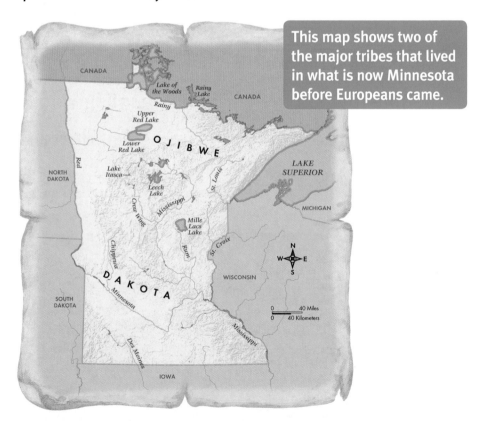

This map shows two of the major tribes that lived in what is now Minnesota before Europeans came.

Ojibwe people made their canoes by stitching together large pieces of bark from local birch trees.

Life in the North

In Minnesota's northern forests, the Ojibwe survived by hunting, fishing, and collecting wild rice. Sometimes they lived in solid, dome-shaped, bark-covered homes called wigwams. Other times they lived in tipis. In summer, they traveled the area's many lakes and waterways using birch-bark canoes. In winter, they used snowshoes and flat sleds called toboggans to get around.

Visitors From Europe

In the 1600s, Europeans arrived in the region. The first to visit were French traders, who came not to settle down but to buy furs. They shipped large bundles of fur back to France and the East Coast. Beaver fur was very popular in Europe and America. The hair was removed from the hide and pressed into felt to make hats. The finest formal top hats were made from beaver fur.

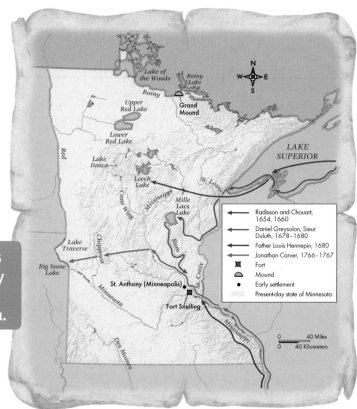

This map shows routes Europeans took as they explored and settled what is now Minnesota.

Today, Fort Snelling is preserved as a National Historic Landmark and open to the public.

Settlers Move In

In 1803, the United States took control of western Minnesota from France as part of the Louisiana Purchase. English-speaking settlers gradually pushed out the French traders and Native Americans. These newcomers came to stay. Instead of furs, they were interested in farming, logging, and mining.

The first permanent U.S. settlement in the region was Fort Snelling. It housed Minnesota's first school, post office, hospital, and military base. In 1858, Minnesota became a U.S. state.

Mill City

The only waterfall on the entire Mississippi River is Saint Anthony Falls. The rushing water was used to power dozens of flour mills as the city of Minneapolis grew up around the falls. Minneapolis became known as the flour milling capital of the world. By 1870, more than 500 mills were grinding wheat into flour all over the state. Sawmills also cut trees from Minnesota's forests into boards.

Timeline of Minnesota Events

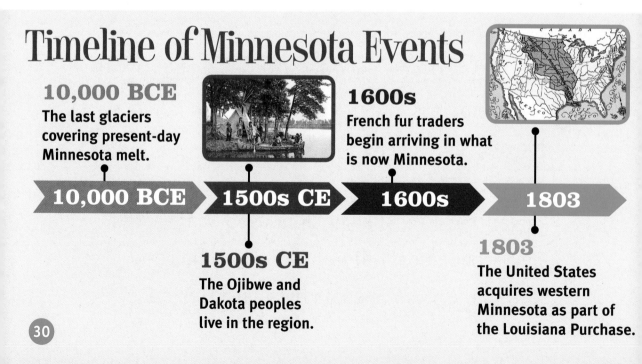

10,000 BCE
The last glaciers covering present-day Minnesota melt.

1600s
French fur traders begin arriving in what is now Minnesota.

10,000 BCE ⟩ 1500s CE ⟩ 1600s ⟩ 1803

1500s CE
The Ojibwe and Dakota peoples live in the region.

1803
The United States acquires western Minnesota as part of the Louisiana Purchase.

Rich in Iron

While farmers turned the prairies into farms, loggers were clearing one-third of the state's forests. But the real prize was underground. It turned out that Minnesota contained more iron ore than any other state. The iron was right near the surface, because the glaciers had scraped off the dirt above. Minnesota's iron was crucial to victories in both World War I (1914–1918) and World War II (1939–1945).

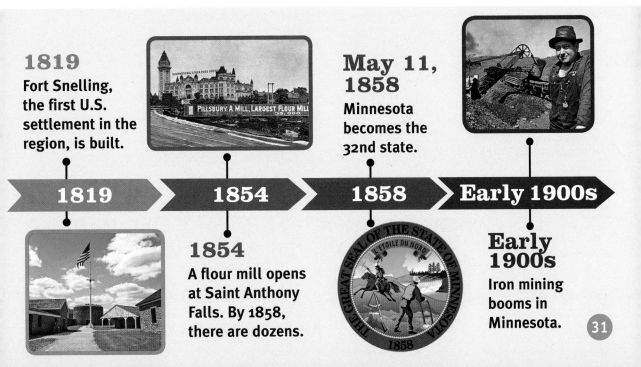

1819
Fort Snelling, the first U.S. settlement in the region, is built.

May 11, 1858
Minnesota becomes the 32nd state.

1819 **1854** **1858** **Early 1900s**

1854
A flour mill opens at Saint Anthony Falls. By 1858, there are dozens.

Early 1900s
Iron mining booms in Minnesota.

31

Fighting for Their Rights

Big businesses often treated loggers, farmers, and miners badly. The workers remained poor while the businesses made millions. Minnesota workers responded by starting their own political party, the Farmer-Labor Party. During the 1930s, this party controlled most key offices in the state. In 1944, it merged with the Democratic Party. The Democratic-Farmer-Labor Party (DFL) fights for civil rights, workers' rights, the environment, and other **liberal** causes.

A poster advertises the Farmer-Labor Party's candidates for the 1936 elections in Minnesota.

Embracing Diversity

Minnesotans have a proud history of supporting equal rights and embracing **diversity**. They showed this again in 2006 by electing the first-ever Muslim member of the U.S. Congress, Keith Ellison. Ellison is also the first African American congressperson to come from Minnesota. He supports **progressive** causes like higher pay for low-income workers. He believes the government should provide health care for all, saying, "I believe universal health care coverage is the civil rights issue of our time."

Saint Paul's annual Hmong American New Year event draws huge crowds to celebrate Hmong traditions and culture.

Culture

Minnesotans love the outdoors. But the cold winters are a good time for indoor activities such as knitting and woodworking. Other traditional crafts include rosemaling, a style of Norwegian decorative painting. Many Hmong people live in Minnesota. This Asian culture is famous for colorful embroidery. Those who just want to look at art instead of making it can visit the Walker Art Center or the Minneapolis Institute of Art. Together these museums attract over a million people each year.

Sports and Outdoor Fun

Minnesotans enjoy their home state's **abundant** ice and snow on skis, snowshoes, and snowmobiles. Minnesota produces more professional hockey players than any other state.

Fans of football, baseball, hockey, and basketball root for the Vikings, Twins, Wild, and Timberwolves. The most successful team in recent years is in women's professional basketball. From 2011 to 2017, the Minnesota Lynx reached the Women's National Basketball Association finals six times and won four championships.

The Minnesota Lynx won the WNBA championship in 2011, 2013, 2015, and 2017.

The first Minnesota State Fair took place in 1859. The event has been held almost every year since then.

A State Fair Like No Other

About two million people go to the Minnesota State Fair each year, making it one of the biggest festivals in the country. The fair offers something for everybody. It has rides, rock concerts, and 15,000 animals. Many people come just for the food. Vendors compete to come up with the wackiest, tastiest snacks. Past treats include walleye on a stick, spaghetti on a stick, and deep-fried fruit.

The Mayo Clinic is famous for its cutting-edge medical procedures and high-tech equipment.

The Working Life

Minnesota has some of America's most productive farms. The state turns out corn, wheat, dairy products, turkeys, and more. Most Minnesotans work in other industries, however. The Mayo Clinic, in Rochester, employs thousands of doctors and researchers. The state is also a leader in high-tech medical devices. While Minnesota still produces more than half of the nation's iron, most mining jobs have disappeared. Today, more people work in tourism than mining.

From Mining to Mountain Biking

In 1984, the last iron mine near the town of Ironton shut down. Local people wondered what could be done to make up for the lost jobs. The once-busy mines left big holes in the ground. But these holes had filled with water, creating lovely lakes surrounded by rocky cliffs. Why not create a giant park? Today, mountain bikers ride trails around the lakes. Boaters paddle kayaks. Scuba divers explore the clear, deep water. Best of all, tourists come for vacations, providing many new jobs to Ironton's people.

Changing Tastes

Until recently, most Minnesotans came from European countries such as Germany, Sweden, and Norway. Their traditional foods remain popular. But today, immigrants from places such as Cambodia, Somalia, and Central America offer many tasty new food options. Still, old-fashioned midwestern meals like hotdish remain popular and are warm, filling, and easy to make.

Tuna Hotdish

Ask an adult to help you!

This classic midwestern dish is the perfect comfort food for a cold night.

Ingredients
1 can cream of mushroom soup
1 can tuna
1 cup frozen peas
1 package frozen tater tots

Directions
Preheat the oven to 350°F. Mix the soup, tuna, and peas in a greased baking pan. Cover with the tater tots. Bake for 40 minutes. Enjoy!

A figure skater takes advantage of a frozen Minnesota lake to practice her routine.

"Minnesota Nice"

Minnesotans are proud of their cold winters. They like to say that toughing it out through the frozen weather builds character. And they may be right! The phrase "Minnesota nice" refers to their good-natured approach to life. The positive attitude of Minnesotans and the state's beautiful setting make Minnesota a wonderful place to visit and live. ★

Famous People

Laura Ingalls Wilder

(1867–1957) wrote *Little House on the Prairie* and other classic children's books. Her childhood home in Walnut Grove is now a museum.

Sinclair Lewis

(1885–1951) was the first American to win the Nobel Prize in Literature. His novel *Main Street* describes life in a small town much like Sauk Centre, where he grew up.

F. Scott Fitzgerald

(1896–1940) was a novelist from Saint Paul who wrote the classic novel *The Great Gatsby*. The book centers on a mild-mannered man from the Midwest who enters a world of glamour and wealth in New York, much like Fitzgerald himself did.

Wanda Gág

(1893–1946) was an artist from New Ulm who wrote and illustrated children's books. In classic books such as *Millions of Cats*, her vibrant drawings seem full of life.

Judy Garland

(1922–1969) was a singer and movie star from Grand Rapids. She is still beloved today for her role as Dorothy in *The Wizard of Oz*.

Charles Schulz

(1922–2000) wrote and illustrated the comic strip *Peanuts* for nearly 50 years. The world he created was filled with unforgettable characters like Charlie Brown and Snoopy. Schulz was a native of Minneapolis.

Bob Dylan

(1941–) started out as a folk singer and then became a rock star. He grew up in Hibbing. His songs are so powerful and original that he won a Nobel Prize in Literature.

Alan Page

(1945–) played in four Super Bowls with the Minnesota Vikings. In 1971, he became the first defensive player to be named Most Valuable Player in the National Football League. He became a lawyer while still playing football and went on to become a justice on the Minnesota Supreme Court.

Prince

(1958–2016) was a singer, songwriter, and musician from Minneapolis. He sold over 100 million albums of his unique blend of rock, pop, funk, soul, and R&B.

Keith Ellison

(1963–) is the first Muslim to serve in the U.S. Congress and the first African American to represent Minnesota in the House of Representatives.

Did You Know That ...

In the winter of 2013–2014, the temperature in the Twin Cities plunged below 0 degrees Fahrenheit (–18 degrees Celsius) 53 times, including 17 days in a row.

One in four Minnesotans has a fishing license.

Waterskiing was invented in Minnesota in 1922 on Lake Pepin, a widened part of the Mississippi River.

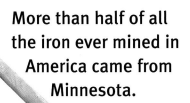

More than half of all the iron ever mined in America came from Minnesota.

More than 65 towns in Minnesota have the word *lake* in their name.

There is one boat for every six people in Minnesota.

Did you find the truth?

(F) The weather in Minnesota is cold year-round.

(T) Minnesota contains the northernmost point in the United States outside Alaska.

Resources

Books

Anastasio, Dina. *Where Is the Mississippi River?* New York: Penguin Workshop, 2017.

Halverson, Alesha. *The Ojibwe: The Past and Present of the Anishinaabe.* Mankato, MN: Capstone Press, 2016.

Heinrichs, Ann. *Minnesota.* New York: Children's Press, 2015.

O'Connor, Jim. *Who Is Bob Dylan?* New York: Penguin Workshop, 2013.

Rozett, Louise (ed.). *Fast Facts About the 50 States: Plus Puerto Rico and Washington, D.C.* New York: Children's Press, 2010.

Visit this Scholastic website for more information on Minnesota:

★ www.factsfornow.scholastic.com
Enter the keyword **Minnesota**

Important Words

abundant (uh-BUHN-duhnt) widely available or present in great quantity

bedrock (BED-rahk) the solid layer of rock under the soil

descendants (dih-SEN-dunts) your descendants are your children, their children, and so on into the future

diversity (dih-VUR-sih-tee) a variety

endangered (en-DAYN-jurd) in danger of becoming extinct, usually because of human activity

glaciers (GLAY-shurz) slow-moving masses of ice found in mountain valleys or polar regions

liberal (LIB-ur-uhl) broad-minded and tolerant of opinions and ideas that are different from your own

progressive (pruh-GRES-iv) in favor of improvement, progress, or reform, especially in political or social matters

woolly mammoths (WUL-ee MAM-uhths) animals that looked like large elephants with long, curved tusks and shaggy hair

Index

Page numbers in **bold** indicate illustrations.

About the Author

Martin Schwabacher is an exhibition writer at the
American Museum of Natural History in New York.
He grew up in Minnesota and returns often for family
vacations on the North Shore of Lake Superior. This
is his 28th book for children.